Vagabonding on a Budget

The New Art of World Travel and True Freedom: Live on Your Own Terms without Being Rich

Written By Robert Vance

© Copyright 2018 by Robert Vance - All rights reserved.

The following eBook is reproduced below with the goal of providing information that is as accurate and reliable as possible. Regardless, purchasing this eBook can be seen as consent to the fact that both the publisher and the author of this book are in no way experts on the topics discussed within and that any recommendations or suggestions that are made herein are for entertainment purposes only. Professionals should be consulted as needed prior to undertaking any of the action endorsed herein.

This declaration is deemed fair and valid by both the American Bar Association and the Committee of Publishers Association and is legally binding throughout the United States. Furthermore, the transmission, duplication or reproduction of any of the following work including specific information will be considered an illegal act irrespective of if it is done electronically or in print. This extends to creating a secondary or tertiary copy of the work or a recorded copy and is only allowed with an expressed written consent from the Publisher. All additional rights reserved.

The information in the following pages is broadly considered to be a truthful and accurate account of facts and as such any inattention, use or misuse of the information in question by the reader will render any resulting actions solely under their purview. There are no scenarios in which the publisher or the original author of this work can be in any fashion deemed liable for any hardship or damages that may befall them after undertaking information described herein.

Additionally, the information in the following pages is intended only for informational purposes and should thus be thought of as universal. As befitting its nature, it is presented without assurance regarding its prolonged validity or interim quality. Trademarks that are mentioned are done without written consent and can in no way be considered an endorsement from the trademark holder.

Table of Contents

Introduction 8

   "What Others Have Done" 9

   "How to Use This Book" 12

   "Coming to a Personal Shift" 14

II: A Whole New Lifestyle 18

   "Introduction to the Concept" 18

   "Make the Most of It!" 20

   "Tips for the Trade" 22

   "Watch out! Warnings for the Experience" 27

   "Take-Aways" 28

III: First Steps 30

   "Introduction to the Concept" 30

   "Make the Most of It!" 31

   "Tips for the Trade" 32

   "Watch out! Warnings for the Experience" 36

   "Take-Aways" 38

IV: On the Road 40

"Introduction to the Concept" 40

"Make the Most of It!" 41

"Tips for the Trade" 45

"Watch out! Warnings for the Experience" 48

"Take-Aways" 51

V: Planting Roots 52

"Introduction to the Concept" 52

"Make the Most of It!" 53

"Tips for the Trade" 55

"Watch out! Warnings for the Experience" 58

"Take-Aways" 60

VI: Back at Home 62

"Introduction to the Concept" 62

"Make the Most of It!" 63

"Tips for the Trade" 64

"Watch out! Warnings for the Experience" 67

"Take-Aways" 70

VII: Conclusion 72

"The Road of Your Life: Here you are now"72

"Moving Forward as a Vagabond" 73

Glossary 75

Introduction

Right before I graduated from college, I felt so eager to leave the small Pennsylvania town where I'd spent the last several years of my life. I didn't really want to go home either, and when I considered the responsibilities that stood before me along with the college loans that were sure to kick in six months after graduation, the only thing that felt right was to travel.

That temptation of utter freedom filled my heart, and my feet were ready to wander. I planned my travels around agricultural opportunities, and I found myself signing up with WWOOF (World Wide Opportunities on Organic Farms) about a month before graduation. I organized one flight to my first destination, and then I left it up in the open.

I knew it was time to travel, but I never realized exactly how much fulfillment those years of travel brought me. At the moment, the liberation of experiencing each state in the United States was intoxicating. Working with the earth in so many different places was absolutely validating. Today, the lessons I learned on the road stayed with me, and I know that I'm forever changed after having withstood the harsh elements, the miles and miles of road, and the trust that the Universe would provide exactly what I needed.

"What Others Have Done"

Many famous people had their own grand adventures of traveling the world and living with hardly any funds. In the 1950s, American Jack Kerouac all but started a movement westward with the Beat Generation. On his infamous journeys with contemporaries Allen Ginsberg, William S. Burroughs, and Gary Snyder, Kerouac praised the open road and the opportunities it can provide. Kerouac and his buddies spent months on the road at a time yet over the years, they kept coming back to the experience of radical travel as a way to get in touch with their deepest and truest roots.

Later, in the 1990s, another American named Chris McCandless took radical travel to a whole new degree. Like me, McCandless graduated from college and immediately took to the road. He rubber-tramped for a while before realizing his ultimate goals were to live as simply and as much off the land as he could. He survived in the wild for a while, but his approach was unsustainable. He eventually died from complications involved with living off the land in the Alaskan wilderness.

As globalism sets into the world, transcontinental travel becomes more achievable by the day, and many people today seem to take advantage of these options more and more. People like Irishwoman Dervla Murphy have been playing this world travel game for much longer, however. Murphy is an inspiring and tireless biker whose travels have created enough content to fill 24 books on her experiences. This extreme minimalist only ever packs one change of clothes and a game to bring on her travels, preferably Scrabble. Although Murphy is in her eighties, she's been to over 50 countries, and she continues her work cycling over the world to this day.

Influencers on social media love to post about their experiences with travel, too. It seems everyone worth following has a meaningful escape once and a while, but not all of these situations actually align with vagabonding. Influencers who actually travel almost constantly, people who live out of their cars and those who seem to have no home and love the freedom are much more in line with what vagabonding actually is. Whether you call it vagabonding, being a nomad, a traveling kid, or a free spirit, this book will provide the guidelines for achieving exactly what you want on the road with as little as humanly possible.

"How to Use This Book"

This book is divided into five main chapters with five sections in each chapter. Each chapter signifies a different stage in your journey, but all five sections cover the same types of information each time. The first chapter "A Whole New Lifestyle" approaches the mentality needed to be a vagabonder. The second discusses your "First Steps" for embarking on your journey, and the third chapter talks about what happens when you actually get "On the Road." Chapter four gets into "Planting Roots" in any place you happen to stay for a few weeks or longer, and the final chapter addresses what it's like when it's all over and you're "Back at Home."

In each of these five chapters, the same sections appear. Always coming first will be the section called "Introduction to the Concept." This section is rather straightforward according to its title, but it essentially addresses the basics. The second section, "Make the Most of It," goes through some of the great things that you can hope to experience as well as some of the struggles you may come up against.

The third section shares "Tips for the Trade" for vagabonders, including adjustment techniques if certain things aren't working for you and pointers for budgeting on the road. The fourth section, "Watch out! Warnings for the Experience" is pretty straightforward as well, but it goes into detail about those things that could threaten your well-being. Finally, the fifth section summarizes what the chapter has shared and brings forth a handful of takeaways that assess what you will learn from each situation. At the very end of this book, you'll find some last-minute tips along with a glossary that goes over any terms you may not recognize.

Whatever stage of the journey you're at, you can choose a setting chapter you need information on and go to whatever section suits your desires and needs. You could easily also read through the book in preparation for your travels. Use this book however you need to and get excited because you really do have a lot to look forward to.

"Coming to a Personal Shift"

You're at the point in your life where you feel everything starting to change. You're questioning the value of material possessions and the issues of worth entwined within the capitalist system we inhabit. You're ready to see landscapes and states and even countries that you've never seen before. You're ready to have the types of conversations you used to only dream about when you meet new people day after day. You're ready to do all this, and that means accepting what has to be left behind so that you can fill that space with adventure.

You're doubting the value of cash and praising the process of a simpler life. You're dreading the concrete jungle and aching to be deep in a whole different environment. You're tired of stagnation, and you feel drawn to the types of experiences you can't have where you've always lived. It's time to hit the road, and it's been a long time coming. You long for the purest experiences you can find with open landscapes, the smell of the road, and your own two feet.

You might not actually be hitchhiking or backpacking in your vagabonding experience this time, but those expressions of trust in the world are preferred if you can feel safe doing so. Regardless of how you do it, you're about to enter a period of travel where your choices will have to be as deliberate as possible, because you'll be focusing your energy on ideas and interactions rather than things for maybe the first time in your life. You will have to slow down and re-learn how to look at the world, and you will have to open up and allow your experiences to teach you sometimes difficult lessons.

As you begin your journey as a vagabonder, you might have the sense that things will never be the same for you ever again – and that is true to a certain degree. You will grow like a flower blooming in daylight, a snake shedding its old skin, or a butterfly emerging from its cocoon. And by the end of your travels, you will hold onto a mindset that stays with you forever, and you will thank your chance with luck and your strength of will for all it allows you to do.

II: A Whole New Lifestyle

"Introduction to the Concept"

Starting out on the journey requires the right amount of mental preparation. Some people aren't ready to let go of the so-called value of money quite yet. Others are still stuck to their possessions. Everyone should always do a good bit of research before they decide where to go and how to get there, so getting ready for the adventure constitutes a step in the journey itself.

Before you begin or take your first step on the road, you'll need to check in with your attitudes, perspectives, and values. You'll also need to fully embrace the truth of vagabonding, which is that even when you're not traveling, the mindset of a vagabonder remains. The true vagabonder embodies an attitude of adventure and imbues everything they do with that spirit. In this chapter, we'll troubleshoot your mindset to make things a little smoother for when you're ready to embark.

We'll also go over some budgeting techniques to get you where you want to be in self-sustainability for your vagabonding exploits, and we'll address how concerned you should be about keeping in touch with friends and family back home once you do set out.

By the end of this chapter, you should feel affirmed in your leanings to go out on the road. You should be confident that this path is the right one for you, and your overall attitudes will be more aligned with your mission, too. You should feel propelled to work on your savings and your health so that you can accomplish as much as possible when you set out into the world. You should be ready to start some serious planning.

"Make the Most of It!"

As you consider your life and what you want it to be, think deeply about your own personal values. What has always been important to who you are, and what feels superficial? How strong do you feel? How independent, and how brave? How important is money to you, really, and how much are you beginning to doubt that value? Conduct this inner analysis with purpose, for you have to know where you stand to be able to shift things in the right way of thinking for the future you hope to achieve.

As a future vagabonder – or as a vagabonder about to hit the road again – remember how much these experiences out in the world can bring you! You're about to slow down the pace of your life and open up to seeing so much more than normal. You'll meet incredible people and do amazing things when you learn to take each day at a time in a whole new way. On the road, you will have your wits and values tested, and you will find yourself feeling free. And you might not have much money all the time, but that will become a valuable experience in and of itself. Through your experiences vagabonding, you will learn again every day how time constitutes true wealth.

Before you head out on the road, you need to accept these big mental shifts, some of which may be entirely new for you and some of which might be incredibly familiar. The two primary changes you'll need to incorporate into your thought processes are that travel is freedom and that money is not true prosperity. Before you head out on the road, practice these beliefs in your life. Whenever you have the chance, question if the ways you're spending your time bring you joy or strife. Question, too, whether you feel free living the routine of your daily life. The more you allow your vagabonding interests to peek through, the more and more ready you'll be to embark when it's time.

One other thing you should do before you set your plans in motion would be to think of those great places in your country or continent or the world that you've always wanted to see. You can dream big with your vagabonding and start off with a thousand great locations to visit, for when it comes down to the real experience, you'll do what you can, and it always helps to have options. Think of a few great places to see, or simply consider the countries you'd like to visit and do some research on their most interesting landmarks.

"Tips for the Trade"

<u>On saving beforehand</u> – You'll want to have a decent amount of money saved before you hit the road, but that will mean different things for people at different stages on the vagabonder's path. Famous vagabonders have traveled with just a backpack of necessities for months at a time with a minimal amount of money. And as you will also be working to remember what's really valuable and what's not, preparing to embark may mean asking yourself some difficult questions. How much money does it take to maintain your home and habits each month? How much are your bills? Your car payment? Your weekly and monthly expenditures to decorate and renovate? You'll likely find that there are things you're spending money on that can be cut down and redirected to your travels. In time, you will eventually realize that any abilities to save beforehand are helpful but unnecessary, for the vagabonder's life is about interacting with all the elements of the world, so time and

other people will become your greatest resource of all when you go abroad.

<u>On fitness beforehand</u> – You'll also want to make sure you're at an adequate level of fitness before you leave for several reasons. First, you need to be realistic about what you're up against in the world, and that means knowing that you may have to run away from danger and that you'll have to be healthy enough to do so. Second, you should be able to withstand a lot of time on your feet, and if you attempt leather tramping, rubber tramping, and hitchhiking at all, you'll need to be able to walk and support your own backpack for miles at a time. Third, your greatest resource when you're staying in a place for a while will be your own body. You'll be able to find work helping people with odd jobs, and you'll be spending lots of your free time experiencing all the local nature has to offer. Before you leave, therefore, it may be helpful to enact a healthful

routing into your life. That may entail changing your diet, but it should definitely involve walking at least 30 minutes. Ideally, you'd go to the gym or go running, but if you can't afford that, go somewhere you can walk safely and build your body up one step at a time.

<u>Keeping in touch back home</u> – Before you go out on the road, set plans with friends and family regarding how often you'll keep in contact. Touching in every single day can be exhausting or impossible for some vagabonders, depending on the places in the world where they currently find themselves. Ideally, you'll be able to connect with the important people in your life once a week and that may mean different things per the group to whom you're reaching out. With family, a phone call is always preferred, and if you're going somewhere where phones won't be able to be used, be sure to tell family beforehand.

With friends, texts through WhatsApp or any other global messaging service are good, but you know they want to see pictures of your life! The best expression here might be a post of several photos at the end of each week to social media to update everyone you care about (and enter them into the vagabonder's way of life, too). With family, set up a fall-back plan so that they'll know what to do if they don't hear from you for a while. If you're traveling alone, let them know loosely where and when you'll be at each place so they can alert the local authorities if things get sketchy. If you're going with someone else or a group, share that person's name and number with your family right off the bat. You'd be surprised how much that can help.

<u>Research other peoples' experiences</u> – To prepare yourself for the exciting and scary realities of life on the road, don't simply replace them with a dreamy and uninformed

idealism. Do some research! Go ahead and read some fellow vagabonders' blogs! Look into situations you're fearful of and arm yourself with information. If you're unsure about traveling alone as a woman or LGBTQ individual, check out some blogs oriented towards the specific perspective you have. I promise they're out there! Reach about other peoples' experiences; take notes if you like. You'll find a wealth of information through this method of research, and you may be surprised what it does for you when the time comes.

"Watch out! Warnings for the Experience"

Two main warnings for this stage both involve your attitude in relation to your upcoming adventure. Be sure to check-in with your attitude over time. It helps to know how you're feeling about your journey and your possessions, for any experience vagabonding can help heal a materialist. Still, you'll be surprised how better off you'll be once you're mentally prepared for some of the most trying and fulfilling moments of your life.

When you're approaching the lifestyle, values, and attitudes of the vagabonder, don't let yourself get caught up on restrictions of age. Remember Dervla Murphy! No matter what age you're at, the true vagabonder is an adventurer at heart and feels full by life in the world. They aim for valuable interactions with others and seeing new landscapes fills them with bliss. Age doesn't restrict you from a life like the vagabonder's – it's all in your mindset and whether you're ready to go out once again and take on the world.

"Take-Aways"

When you look back on these times of preparation and evaluation after your travels, you will see them glistening with potential. You'll always remember them fondly, and as you're living these moments now, remember to make the most of them! Enjoy the research you get to do and let yourself feel excited about your future travels! If you're not quite at the point with the mindset yet that you need to be, look at each experience as practice for how things will be. Try to consciously approach each moment as a teaching experience or a chance to say goodbye to something you'll not have in your life for a while. Whether that means friends and family, pets, places, or things, take time to say goodbye and relish in the love that's shared at these gatherings. If you get homesick later, these instances in memory can help fuel you. How incredible is the power of love shared?

III: First Steps

"Introduction to the Concept"

Getting ready to leave can be the most anxiety-ridden part of your journey. You'll need to figure out some of your plans, establish a method of travel, re-establish your mindset, affirm some type of money pool as back up, prepare your food supply, and then get your feet going. For some, this process is a lot, but for the vagabonder, you don't really need as much as you think you do.

In this chapter, you'll learn some techniques for slimming down your supply and packing as smart as possible. You'll also need to change your bodily rhythms if you've been hopped up on coffee and rush logic for quite some time, so we'll also go over how you can tone things down before you move on out.

Before this chapter ends, you should have some concrete plans in place for your journey, and you should have a much better sense of what to pack. You'll have a good degree of anxiety relieved through this process, and your confidence will help give you the boost needed to put in your two weeks' notice at work or buy that first bus ticket.

"Make the Most of It!"

When you look forward to your next grand adventure, you'll need some idea of where to go. That list of countries, landmarks, locations, and cities you've always wanted to see from earlier can be of real help here. When you get in the mood to set some plans, use this previous list as your guidelines. From that list, you can tell generally what countries you want to go to, and from the landmarks, you can tell what parts of those countries you want to be in. Furthermore, you should always think about seasonal complications because some places are inaccessible at certain times of the year, while other landmarks and famous sites are most beautiful at other times.

Do the research, expend the forethought, and draw out a map! Your journey will be all the more fruitful with a few solid plans in place, and if you really want to, just go for it with as little planning as possible, there are still a few helpful and minimal plans you can make that will at least give ease to your family and friends. Even if it's just noting your general path from home or a few locations you will definitely see, a small plan can provide enough structure and wiggle room to produce incredibly creative and life-changing moments.

"Tips for the Trade"

Break your home habits – There are surely routines in your life that you won't be able to bring on the road. You won't be able to take all those luxuries with you, and that will be absolutely incredible. You'll get to embrace what will grow in the spaces left empty when all these things change. These experiences might grow new habits, might completely destroy old habits, might adapt old routines, and might help you become stronger. You will learn to adapt, and sometimes, that means cutting a habit completely, while other times, it means you need to get a little creative. Try cutting the coffee and switching to tea steeped in a glass pot of water set in direct sunlight: sun tea! Try turning off the TV or Netflix and switching to that exercise routine we talked about. Try deleting some apps and working on a creative project instead.

On packing intelligently – You won't be able to bring much on your journey, so you'll have to be smart about how you pack. If you bring more than one change of clothes, try rolling up the clothes instead of folding them. There are plenty YouTube tutorials that instruct on how to make the most clothes seem the fewest in packing, so feel free to check those out. You could also just pack *fewer* clothes instead. Remember Dervla? She always only brought one change of clothes, and famous vagabonder Rolf Potts notoriously only brought two or three. When packing clothes, remember *you don't need as much as you think*. For utensils and tools, try to find a multitool that seems sturdy and effective. Bring items that accomplish several different means at once. Consider solar-powered technologies to eliminate the need for charging cables and cords. Cut out the excess, and you'll be surprised what you have space for.

What to bring/what not to bring – You'll also have to practice efficiency, minimalism, and selectivity in *what* you pack. If you'll be backpacking, you can't just bring everything that fits. You have to be economical with weights and pressures that you place on your body, for if you overexert yourself in a style of living that depends on the powers and strength of your body, you'll end up screwed. A few tips for what to bring are as follows. Ditch the books and grab yourself an eBook reader. Borrow one from a friend if you can't afford it! If you have no other option but to bring your own books, choose two or three of the best options for the sake of weight. Go for light fare instead of heavy stuff. Even your backpack itself should be light. Your jacket – if you need one – should also be light and incredibly efficient. Ditch the umbrella and pack some light-weight ponchos. Go for a sleeping pad or hammock instead of a full-on sleeping bag. Bring granola bars and snacks instead of dehydrated meals or bigger items. And always remember to do research on what places around your destinations have free food options or incredibly cheap prices. They will be essential for your longevity on the road as well as the lightness of your pack.

"Watch out! Warnings for the Experience"

Once again, there are two primary warnings about the experience of setting things in motion. The first one aligns with our warnings about coffee before. You may be overly indoctrinated in the lifestyle of *fast*: fast food, fast turnovers at work, fast meetings, fast mornings, and days that pass by without notice. You might be drinking excessive amounts of coffee or caffeine to get through your days, and that approach won't be helpful at all in your travels. Make sure you learn to slow down before you leave.

The second warning references your place of work. In order to sustain the lifestyles of the vagabond, you *might* be able to put your job on hold, but this action could entail quitting your job for many readers. In these moments, remember that there *will* be other jobs, and if you're not interested in going back to that work world, remember to embrace the absolute *elation* of true freedom. Breathe in a sigh of relief and tell yourself that it all will really be okay.

As you become entrenched in the vagabonding mindset, you'll find that the Universe really does provide exactly what you need to succeed, and that will mean either finding validity and sustenance through a new style of living, or it can even mean that your experiences on the road point you in the direction of the perfect new job exactly when you come to need it. If you have to quit your job, feel as confident as possible in your decision. Share your opinions and needs with your boss, too. Being as open and honest will benefit your situation. You're actively putting your behaviors in line with your attitudes and values, and that's commendable to anyone. Go ahead and put in your two weeks' notice. Find yourself a replacement if need be. Just do it and wait to see what good comes to pass.

"Take-Aways"

Try not to be afraid as you take these first steps towards your vagabonding goals. Try to remember that you're bringing power and strength into your life with every decision you make and don't let yourself get too caught up in anxieties if you can help it. In general, this chapter should have taught you the value of minimalism on the road, and you should feel like you have a better sense of what to pack and what to leave behind. After you have all your first steps completed and your mindset is all lined up with your future adventure, you'll be ready to hit the road, and that will be one of the most rewarding moments you ever experience in your entire life. I hope you're looking forward to it because your life is about to be changed forever.

IV: On the Road

"Introduction to the Concept"

You've made it! You're actually on the road! You're relying on your feet, your wheels, your people, your backpack, new friends, and only your most absolutely necessary possessions as you proceed from here on out. This chapter will help you deal with some of the most common issues for people who've both just started traveling as well as for those who've been doing so quite a while. We'll touch on protecting your energy, making the right choices, and budgeting on a rush. There will also be a few ideas about where you can go and what you can do when you're traveling on low funds.

Before the end of this chapter, you should feel that you can do anything you choose and that it will be done safely and smartly. You should be more confident in your ability to make the *right* choices, too, for that will provide confidence and backbone to your smart and safe mission. You should also feel more comfortable living your life primarily on the road, so you should be starting to consider your options when it comes to planting new roots as your journey continues.

"Make the Most of It!"

As you live out completely new circumstances and experiences through your travels on the road, always remember to make the most of your experiences. A few tips may help in this endeavor. You might get tired of constantly thinking of where to go next, and there are a few types of spaces you can look to consistently for new ideas. Wherever you are, try going to a nearby nature reserve or even a public park, seek out niche bookstores or record stores, look for shops that are like nothing you've ever seen before and checked them out for yourself, research spaces that are packed with history and spend the day exploring, or even seek out the oldest building in town and make your way to its splendor.

If you're more of a social person, try to spend time in coffee shops, bars, or clubs – with the right awareness and sense of security so that nothing bad happens either. You could seek out Meetup groups in the area or make friends through couch-surfing sites. In the modern world, the number of apps is endless. You could download the Meetup app and find groups of people to hang out with the same interests towards a topic or focus, and you can message anyone around the world through WhatsApp and other similar applications. You could download the Couchsurfing app and find places to stay for free anywhere. You could also try any language-related apps to help you learn and translate in spaces where you're not fluent. You could also make connections through WWOOFing as I did in my own travels, or you could hang out in libraries to get a sense of the local vibe.

Wherever you find yourself, don't be afraid to make friends and share information about your travels, theirs, and techniques for success. By bonding with other vagabonders and locals, you will find a wealth of knowledge you may have never considered yourself. The more friends you make – virtually and IRL – the more options you'll have for sleeping, eating, community-building, and local learning. These people will also give you direction for places to see and cultural events to experience. They'll encourage you to take those plans you made and scrap them! And this is the gist of true adventuring. Let the course take you wherever it does and let people into your life on the way for added bonuses. Wherever you find yourself and whatever you find yourself doing, remember to fully live it and slow down so you can retain these memories for a lifetime.

When you accrue friends like this in each place, travel together, and share your information, you'll find that your travels in the future benefit as well. In your journey, you can always see where your other vagabonding friends are and plan meet-ups and reunion tours along the way. There will be a thousand experiences that present them to you, but you should still remember to be smart and make educated choices. Just because you've met someone, and they suggest an adventure does not mean you should jump right in. Stay cautious and trust your intuition with new friends. Done well, this attitude can save your life.

"Tips for the Trade"

<u>On budgeting</u> – When it comes to budgeting on the road, you might find yourself facing the urge to splurge. At bars and coffee shops, you can make connections and soak up Wi-Fi, but you also potentially waste your funds on something superficial that's not needed. If you put yourself in these locations, however, that's clearly not a bad thing. Just try to get the cheapest possible option – buy just an espresso or a domestic beer instead of a fancy drink or cocktail. Budgeting can be broken down very easily if you find ways to sleep outside as much as possible. The true vagabonder wants to be in communion with nature, and they would find absolute joy in being able to sleep outside every night. If you're not there yet with your vagabonding energies, don't stress – hostels still exist, and they're always an affordable option, but you might want to try to shift your thinking over

time to connect better with your local environments if you can. You're going for minimalism and low trace in the world, so this way of being is aligned with your values – you just have to work on that mindset a bit first.

On routine – It may seem impossible to incorporate routine in your travels, but I guarantee it's possible and it's productive. Try to include routine into your daily expression when possible, whether that means regularly spaced-out walks for your dog each day or to develop certain morning habits wherever you are. Your routine may be as basic as waking at dawn and going to sleep during sunset, or it could be as complicated as practicing yoga at dawn followed by sun tea and meditation before doing anything else. In general, grounding practices while traveling will be essential for your overall mental health. If you don't establish a routine or find it impossible to do so, at least try to incorporate one grounding exercise into each day. That could mean stretching, doing yoga, meditating, or keeping a journal – just try something that keeps your sights on your goals and reminds you exactly where and who you are.

On weekly touch-ins with family – It may become cumbersome to entertain your goals of keeping in touch with family and friends weekly, and that's absolutely okay. Just do what you can, and they'll be sure to understand as long as you're honest about what's going on. Sometimes, you just need to go out on your own for a while and do something off-plan. You can still let your family know that you need some time so that they're not concerned. Sometimes, you just forget to be in touch. Before you get to that moment, warn your friends and family that you're getting pretty caught up in the experience and that you might not be able to keep in contact as well as you like. With friends and family back home, the best technique is honesty, especially in times when communication becomes hard.

"Watch out! Warnings for the Experience"

There are two big things you should watch out for on the road. One is dangerous animals and the other is dangerous humans. Dangerous animals are one thing because they're often recognizable as life-threatening, whether it's a domestic dog with rabies or a bear approaching you in the woods. Something, you can do to protect yourself in these situations would be to have pepper spray with you at all times – or even bear spray could help. Keep a whistle near you too, so that you can scare away a hungry and bigger animal that approaches you.

For both dangerous animals and humans, you might also want to carry a weapon or two. You might not feel good about carrying a gun, but they can be life-altering when it comes to your survival on the road. Even Dervla Murphy has a gun when she travels, which she's used to defending her life from ravenous wolves and assaulting men in her travels. You never know when you'll need to show your cards against an assailant but having at least a knife can help you stand your ground.

Overall, you should stay cautious and keep your heart open. You'll want to notice when people pose a threat to you, and that takes equal parts of intellect and intuition. Furthermore, if you're leather tramping or hitchhiking in any capacity, make sure to have your weapon as handy as possible, and don't forget the strength of your voice. As soon as you get in someone else's vehicle, make your situation plain to them – tell them what you're looking for and what you won't allow. Tell them you have a weapon, too, so they take you more seriously.

If you're in a situation with an assailant, don't be afraid to use what you have, whether it be pepper spray, bear spray, a gun, or a knife. You don't have to kill someone to be able to disable them from attacking you, even with a gun, so learning proper technique would be something to work on before you leave, but if you find yourself in a dangerous situation, you should clearly do anything you can to save your own life. If you're a train-riding rubber tramper, always do some research before you get in a train car. Find out where it's going and where it's coming from. You're traveling for liberation, not to bring death upon you sooner, so don't reject research as useless, impure, cheating, or a waste of the vagabond's time. It really can save your life.

"Take-Aways"

When you live the backpacker's life on the road, you will see amazing things. You will learn to trust yourself and others like never before, and you will become the strongest you've been in your entire life. Vagabonding is a beautiful experience that links us with our most advanced potential, and you are encouraged to remember that when times get tough: never forget about your choice to be exactly where you are right now and your power that you grew and harnessed to make that happen.

V: Planting Roots

"Introduction to the Concept"

Sometimes, we get stuck in places for a while when we're vagabonding. Whether it's a few weeks or months or even a series of years, there will be places that draw a tether directly to your heart. For those moments when you do plan to momentarily settle and plant your shallow, nomadic roots, this chapter has a lot to say.

We'll touch on some productive veins of action before addressing a couple things you should always be concerned about. The topics included the range from building relationships and doing the right types of work to engaging with volunteerism, earning funds, and homesickness.

By the end of this chapter, you should feel assured of what you can do when you get stuck somewhere as well as how to make the most of a long stay for weather's sake. You will have techniques for connecting with the locals, and you will even learn about how to build a business wherever you find yourself. In due time, you might find that life on the road is the only one for you. For others, these moments will be a reminder that eventually, you do have to go back home, and they will get you ready once again for that strange transition.

"Make the Most of It!"

When you end up planting roots on your adventure, whether by choice, by fate, or by the fault of weather, you'll need to know how to make the most of your experiences in stasis after living life in flux for so long. A few techniques to help you do exactly that are to make friends with your neighbors and try out some local volunteer work.

Even if you don't speak the local language, reach out to the people living around you. Not being able to understand one another isn't the worst problem you could experience, especially given that all earthlings tend to use the same gestures, and even the most terrible artists can scratch down a map or an image for reference. Let go of your reservations, get brave, and talk to your neighbors. As with all the people you meet in the world when you're traveling, you'd be surprised the wealth of knowledge those around you contain that can aid your mission and progress.

Additionally, don't be afraid to exert yourself in your local environments. Volunteer in local organizations or do some guerrilla gardening on the local street corner. Look out for

WWOOF farms in your neighborhood or get your hands dirty doing some landscaping or contracting. Get out there and volunteer. By really engaging with the communities where you stop and plant roots, you'll find yourself making friends for a lifetime and being taught lessons that you'd never guessed you could learn.

"Tips for the Trade"

<u>On earning funds</u> – The most likely and the biggest concern that'd lead to your planting roots would probably be that you've run out of funds for your journey. When you're low or out of additional funds, don't fret. There are so many ways you can still follow with your goals and live out this life-changing adventure. It just might mean staying still for a little bit first, however. If you're in a situation where you need to earn funds as soon as possible, my first suggestion would be to let go of that urgency and see what happens. Remember

that money is not the same thing as wealth; time is. If you find yourself with a lot of time on your hands in a new place, just imagine how prosperous you've set yourself up to be. On the one hand, you can reject your impulses to get a job or ask for money from friends and family who may need it. You can choose to live as minimal and as off-the-land as possible. You can choose to engage with people one-on-one for the desires you need to have met. On the other hand, you can go towards work and charity instead of just trusting in the Universe to provide. You can claim agency from your situation and go get that local job! You could volunteer for a local food shelter and receive food that way. Otherwise, you could ask people back home to support you from afar. Asking for help might not be in your nature, but when people receive requests from friends that have been asked earnestly, they respond more positively than poorly. Don't be afraid to ask for exactly what you need, for those things will come, and it'll blow your mind when they do.

On working abroad – If you're in a country where you speak the language, apply for a local job! Go out and try the coffee shops, the libraries, the bookstores, and the bars. Focus your attention to places you know you'll meet people with good connections and life-altering information. Get that temporary job that can help you get to the next place, but always be honest with your employers about your intention. Let them know you're traveling and just stopping through! That expression will help you weed out employers that won't work with you as well as opportunities that are too long-term to learn well quickly. Furthermore, that expression will give you the chance to meet people who already know you to a certain extent and feel connected to your journey. To have people on your side in a foreign state or country may mean all the difference when it comes to going back home.

"Watch out! Warnings for the Experience"

When you're planting these temporary or shallow roots, there are two things to be aware of that might hinder your progress. Opposing experiences of homesickness and cold feet can come upon you at any time, and they'll make your stay rough for a while until you're able to unpack the emotions and settle into a new and profound comfort with being exactly where you are now.

The vagabonder's greatest enemy on the road is homesickness. Homesickness will keep you from exploring your current destination, it will keep you from meeting new people, and it will keep you from enjoying the opportunities that surround you. If you're stuck with a tough batch of homesickness, the first step is realizing that you're living in the past and future. Vagabonding is about embracing the present, and you will find yourself paralyzed from being able to do that as long as you wallow with homesickness. Instead of wallowing, go outside and practice a distracting activity. Go out and find someplace that's nothing like your home and write down five things about it that feel incredible to withstand. For experiences with homesickness, let yourself feel the sadness and the loss, but don't get stuck on them. Rather than get caught in that emotional mud, keep your energies focused upon the next great thing. With an open mind and a sense of adventure, no batch of homesickness could ever keep you down.

With cold feet, on the other hand, building foundations anywhere will be difficult because you can't imagine staying still for long enough for it to become a home. You might be so eager to travel and continue your adventure that even weather-induced stays feel torturous and oppressive. For those with cold feet who'd rather keep moving and moving, remember what good can come from planting roots. You might need to stay for just a few nights to meet the person who'll change your life forever. The Universe is funny and ironic like that. Wherever you find yourself, always try to be fully there for as long as you have to stay. The feelings of having cold feet won't disappear, but you'll learn to live with them and turn that fizzling, sparky energy into something you can use in time. Simply be patient and trust that you're exactly where you need to be for the moment. Breathe, and ground yourself in the *now*. Those cold feet might get warm after all.

"Take-Aways"

For those times when you get stuck, for those times when the weather inhibits your movement, for those times when your funds run out, and for those times when you just have to stay still for a moment, this chapter can make all the difference. As long as you're remembering to get invested in your local communities, make friends, and establish new relationships, there's no way why this "stuck" feeling can't aid in your overall growth. As long as you inhabit the *now* wherever you are, with whomever you're with, you practice the vagabond's way, and you flourish with each breath you breathe.

VI: Back at Home

"Introduction to the Concept"

Returning home after extended time away can be harder to adjust to than you think. If you've been backpacking, rubber tramping, or leather tramping, you might have a difficult time remembering where you are every time you wake up from sleep. For all vagabonders though, the adjustment back to standard time isn't always that simple.

In this chapter, we'll remind ourselves how to maintain the vagabonder's mindset even after coming back to a stable and housed situation. We'll also discuss how to plan more travel into your future so that you can keep this engagement with the world in active practice. By the end of this chapter, you should feel affirmed in your potential to grow anywhere, and you should have processes in place to help your house feel like home once more. If you sold your home and gave up your job to travel instead, this chapter should allow you to feel affirmed that anywhere can be *home* – it just matters how you practice grounding, home-ing, and vagabonding as your path continues.

"Make the Most of It!"

Even when you're back home, you can work on enhancing the vagabonder's mindset for application in day-to-day tasks. You can remember to approach every interaction, every project, every task assigned at your job, and every moment of travel as if it's a full-on adventure. You can keep those same values of friendship and community when you go back home, too, which means that what you learned on the road will come back and help boost the world you had to leave behind for a time. Everything comes full circle like this on the road.

When you're back at home, don't forget to make the most of the experience by seeking out nature adventures whenever you can, even if you didn't use to do that before you left in the first place. Put yourself in situations that remind you of your travels, even if that means going to a different religious worship service or a bar in a new part of town. Seek out new thrills and engage with cultures you may have ignored before. Be conscious and confident when you go to make choices, and always aim for growth. That is the vagabond's way, and you don't need to be currently on the road to embody it.

"Tips for the Trade"

On adjusting – Reworking yourself into your hometown community once again can be complicated. And it could even be that your experiences as a vagabonder caused you to build your home in a place far, far away from your hometown instead. Wherever you've made your home, staying still after what feels like a lifetime of travel is not the easiest task. If you struggle with adjusting back to the calmer lifestyle of "home," you can always try to recall the true mainstay of vagabonding, which is to strive to make every experience, situation, and interaction an adventure. If you're having trouble adjusting into the working life once more, every vagabonder in the world feels for you. It hurts to have to trade the value of time for the value of money after living so freely, but after your experiences in the world, you likely have a better idea of what work would actually help you grow. Now that you return and make your home, you can use this self-knowledge to make sure that if you *do* have to earn money to sustain yourself, at least your job aligns with your truest potential.

<u>On future adventures</u> – If you do have to work and build a home against your hopes and dreams to keep vagabonding, you can use these intermittent "home periods" as a way to boost your energy, morale, and bank account for future adventures on the road. Use these imagined travels as the inspiration to work hard and earn money. Use these future freedoms as justification to work the system again now. Use these vagabond potentials to keep yourself inspired and oriented towards the future you wish to have. Use the liberating planning periods for travel as a way to keep your sanity sitting still so long at work. There are clearly ways to use vagabonding to your advantage at home, and the best one is to use those experiences to propel yourself toward more of the glorious same. And the more vagabonding you do, the more streamlined your approach will be: the less money you'll need, the less planning you'll do, and the less stuff you'll feel compelled to bring along. Each time you come home, you have the ability to

process all that you've learned on the road, and that time is invaluable – even if it doesn't seem so right now.

"Watch out! Warnings for the Experience"

As with each other setting in the vagabond's travels, coming home relates to two more struggles to endure. You'll want to be careful with your recapitulation into everyday time, and you'll also want to establish sleep as a sacred time, as it will be wonky (and strangely insightful) for a while. First, getting reacclimated to the clock and calendar time of the working world won't be easy for some. Vagabonds on the road become used to setting their phones down, telling the time by the sun, learning nature's rhythms, and telling the month by the seasons. Vagabonds can stay reconnected to this larger sense of time when they return home, and they can also relearn to keep the clock in mind.

Essentially, the vagabond's return to society places them in a liminal position in-between here and there, stasis and flux, home and travel, concern and care-free. This liminal position means that clock time meets with the earth's time, and while disorienting, this experience can be one of the greatest teachers of all. You will begin hybridizing your lessons from the road with your work life and relationships at home. You'll enact the vagabonder's mindset wherever you are, so stress and anxiety, societal concerns, and unimportant foci will melt away, leaving the purest intentions, actions, and paths clearer to you than ever before.

Second, the readjustment period back home will mean that waking from sleep may feel somewhat surreal. Sleeping in so many different places leaves your mind a bit fragile upon return, but you can still make use of this jarring feeling. If you ever wake up, see your ceiling, and legitimately wonder where you are or if you wake up and think you're about to awaken into the world of the road, probably in someone else's home (since you feel a bed beneath you), with an unlimited day before you, you aren't going crazy.

This experience is absolutely normal, and you can even glean a few things about your current life and your future on the road by your sights, expectations, and feelings in these strange quasi-lucid, sleep-filled moments. You can consider the place you thought you were about to wake into – maybe you just had a dream about that place, or you're generally feeling drawn back there. You can consider the entire experience as an example of your vagabond instincts in action. There's obviously a part of you that's still ready to explore, still ready to encounter anything new, and you're being drawn back to it intrinsically. Or, you can consider the power that your mind has to create your own reality, for on some level; you were able to believe with your heart you were somewhere else, sometimes, anywhere else. That feeling is so strange and bothersome in part because it's so real for a moment. If that's not proof of the brain's power, I'm not sure what is.

"Take-Aways"

The experience of traveling like a vagabond will affect you forever, and, sometimes, the readjustment period takes a while. Be patient with yourself. Be as honest with your friends and family as possible, and don't blindly fall back into the rut of putting all your energy into just work. Remember the lessons of the road: minimalism, expansion, limitlessness, positive interactivity, exchange, productivity, and more. Channel these lessons into use in your life, and you'll never lose those moments. You'll be forever changed.

VII: Conclusion

"The Road of Your Life: Here you are now"

You're a vagabond for good now, whether you like it or not. You truly *are* forever changed. You now know that what you always dreamed of has been more achievable than you ever imagined, mostly because you've seen it played out in your life. You now know that the vagabond lifestyle not only works but also its attitude help people flourish. You may not always be traveling, but you'll always be continuing down the road of your own life, and you can always practice what vagabonding has taught you. Above all else, wherever you are, fill that moment and that experience with a sense of adventure, and remember to inhabit the *now* of every situation. In time you'll find your joy in life is never-ending because you can take yourself anywhere.

"Moving Forward as a Vagabond"

After I settled back at home from my years-long jaunt vagabonding, I still have the drive to go back. I'm sure I'll get out on the road at some point again, but for now, I'm focusing on reserving my energy, preserving my time, and conserving my money. I'm preparing for the next point of departure as you read, and I hope that you will too, after coming home, return back to the wonder of life that is traveling.

I have a feeling my next step as an American will be outside the continental United States, but I want to make sure that my journey is as conscious and impacting as possible. As I look toward the potential of new times on the road, I aim to leave no trace if I can help it, aside from the making of new friends.

Moving forward as a vagabond sometimes means staying still. There will be moments when you need to plant roots for a while in order to draw sustenance for yourself in one place for an extended period of time. There will be moments when you need to look back to where you have been, and you may even have to literally move back to those places to acquire the energy and inspiration that you need to progress down your personal path once again. The life of the vagabond is constantly in flux, but the values always stay the same. While the sights may change, the heart and the will are always connected and always oriented towards growth. To be a vagabond is to be a spark that becomes a passionate flame. It is to live every day to the fullest and to learn all from life that you can. Burn brightly, vagabond reader, for you light up your own future.

Glossary

a. <u>Backpacker/backpacking</u> – someone whose main source of travel is likely nature paths and roads; travel is made carrying a single backpack of possessions
b. <u>Cold feet</u> – to feel compelled to leave, as if itching to leave a place; also reflects a general inability to commit
c. <u>Couchsurfing</u> – planning your travel around opportunities provided by others you may or may not know who has a couch you could stay on for a night or more
d. <u>IRL</u> – literally "in real life"
e. <u>Leathertramp</u> – to hitchhike (or drive) as a primary mode of travel, which includes lots of time spent walking down highways waiting for your ride to come

f. <u>Rubbertramp</u>– to walk as a primary mode of travel with interludes of hitchhiking; see backpacking
g. <u>Train-rider</u> – someone whose main mode of transportation is to hitch rides on trains, which is illegal in the United States and more legal to perform abroad
h. <u>Vagabonder</u> – someone who lives cheaply, travels often, and always lives with a sense of adventure

www.ingramcontent.com/pod-product-compliance
Lightning Source LLC
Chambersburg PA
CBHW030130100526
44591CB00009B/596